Zbigniew PREISNER's original film music for KIESLOWSKI's Three Co

Arranged for solo piano

Blue   White   Red

Three Colours
Blue

Song For The Unification Of Europe   2
Van Den Budenmayer - Funeral Music   6
Second Flute   8
The Battle Of Carnival And Lent II   7
Olivier's Theme - Finale   10

Three Colours
White

A Chat In The Underground   12
Home At Last   14
On The Wisla   16
Don't Fall Asleep   19
The Party On The Wisla   24
Morning At The Hotel   20

Three Colours
Red

Fashion Show I   27
Do Not Take Another Man's Wife I   32
Fashion Show II   34
Finale   36

Chester Music
part of The Music Sales Group
London / New York / Paris / Sydney / Copenhagen / Berlin / Madrid / Tokyo

Song For The Unification Of Europe from 'Trois Couleurs Bleu'

Composed by Zbigniew Preisner
Arranged by Jack Long

© Copyright 1993 by MK2 - 55, rue Traversière - 75012 Paris - France.
This arrangement © Copyright 2004 by MK2.
All Rights Reserved. International Copyright Secured.

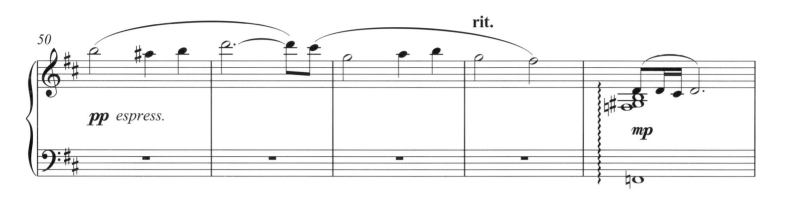

Van Den Budenmayer - Funeral Music from 'Trois Couleurs Bleu'

Composed by Zbigniew Preisner
Arranged by Jack Long

© Copyright 1993 by MK2 - 55, rue Traversière - 75012 Paris - France.
This arrangement © Copyright 2004 by MK2.
All Rights Reserved. International Copyright Secured.

The Battle Of Carnival And Lent II from 'Trois Couleurs Bleu'

Composed by Zbigniew Preisner
Arranged by Jack Long

© Copyright 1993 by MK2 - 55, rue Traversière - 75012 Paris - France.
This arrangement © Copyright 2004 by MK2.
All Rights Reserved. International Copyright Secured.

Second Flute from 'Trois Couleurs Bleu'

Composed by Zbigniew Preisner
Arranged by Jack Long

© Copyright 1993 by MK2 - 55, rue Traversière - 75012 Paris - France.
This arrangement © Copyright 2004 by MK2.
All Rights Reserved. International Copyright Secured.

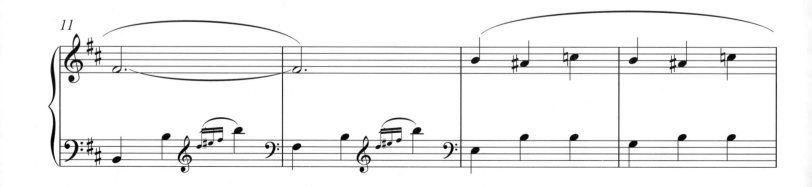

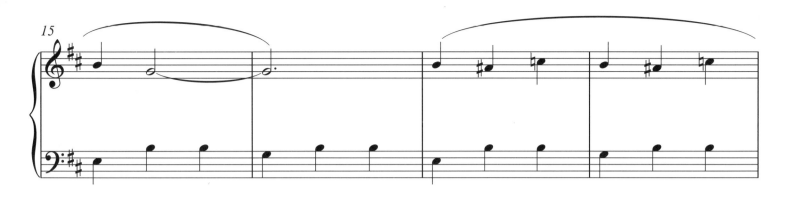

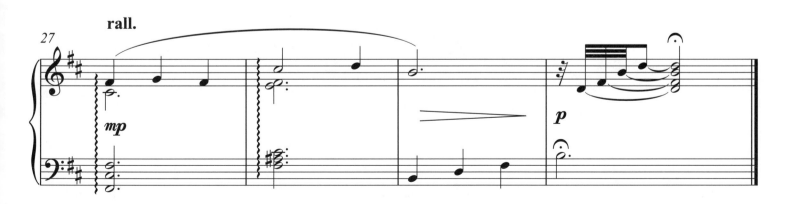

Olivier's Theme - Finale from 'Trois Couleurs Bleu'

Composed by Zbigniew Preisner
Arranged by Jack Long

© Copyright 1993 by MK2 - 55, rue Traversière - 75012 Paris - France.
This arrangement © Copyright 2004 by MK2.
All Rights Reserved. International Copyright Secured.

A Chat In The Underground from 'Trois Couleurs Blanc'

Composed by Zbigniew Preisner
Arranged by Jack Long

© Copyright 1993 by MK2 - 55, rue Traversière - 75012 Paris - France.
This arrangement © Copyright 2004 by MK2.
All Rights Reserved. International Copyright Secured.

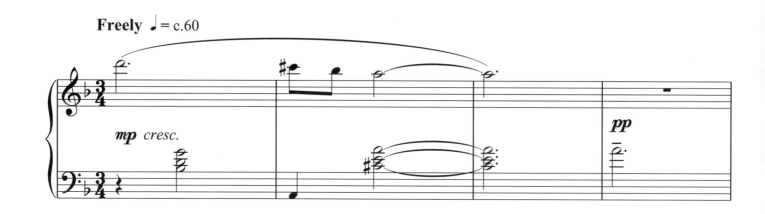

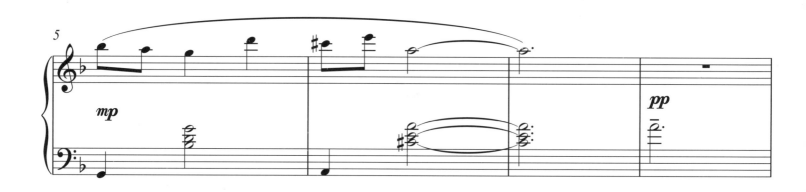

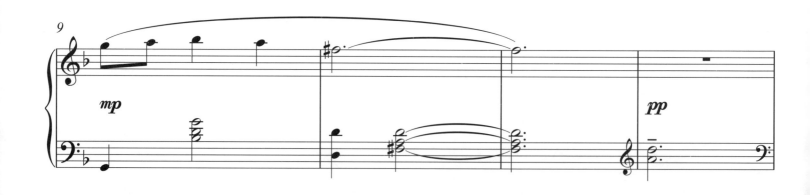

Home At Last from 'Trois Couleurs Blanc'

Composed by Zbigniew Preisner
Arranged by Quentin Thomas

© Copyright 1993 by MK2 - 55, rue Traversière - 75012 Paris - France.
This arrangement © Copyright 2004 by MK2.
All Rights Reserved. International Copyright Secured.

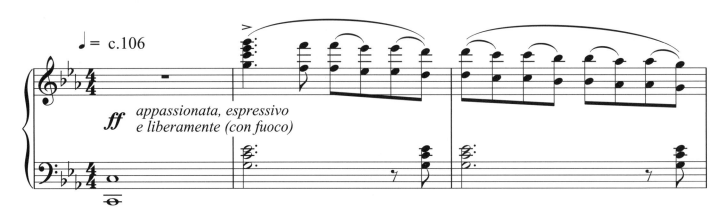
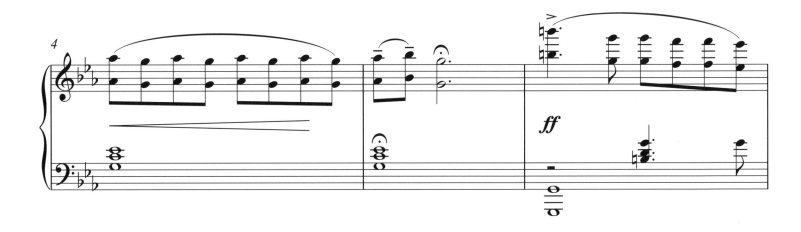
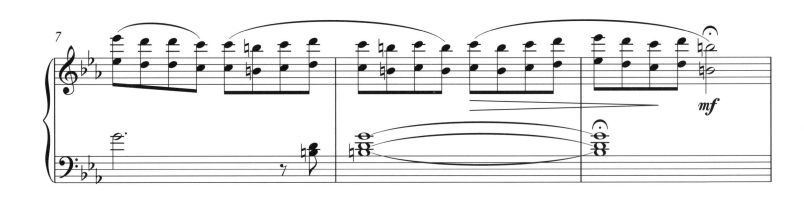
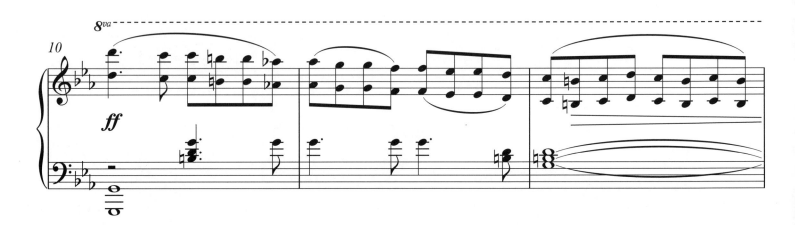

On The Wisla from 'Trois Couleurs Blanc'

Composed by Zbigniew Preisner
Arranged by Jack Long

© Copyright 1993 by MK2 - 55, rue Traversière - 75012 Paris - France.
This arrangement © Copyright 2004 by MK2.
All Rights Reserved. International Copyright Secured.

Don't Fall Asleep from 'Trois Couleurs Blanc'

Composed by Zbigniew Preisner
Arranged by Jack Long

© Copyright 1993 by MK2 - 55, rue Traversière - 75012 Paris - France.
This arrangement © Copyright 2004 by MK2.
All Rights Reserved. International Copyright Secured.

Morning At The Hotel from 'Trois Couleurs Blanc'

Composed by Zbigniew Preisner
Arranged by Quentin Thomas

© Copyright 1993 by MK2 - 55, rue Traversière - 75012 Paris - France.
This arrangement © Copyright 2004 by MK2.
All Rights Reserved. International Copyright Secured.

Slow, quasi Tango

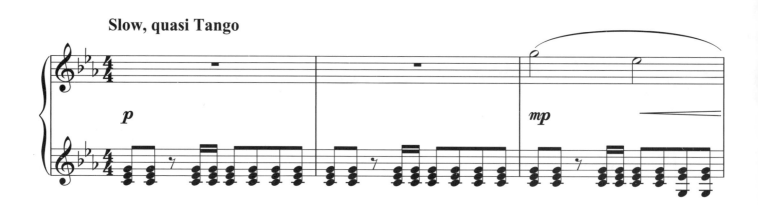
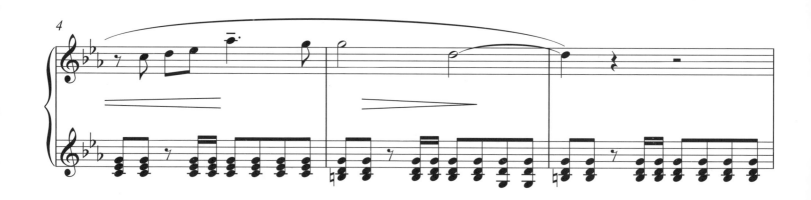

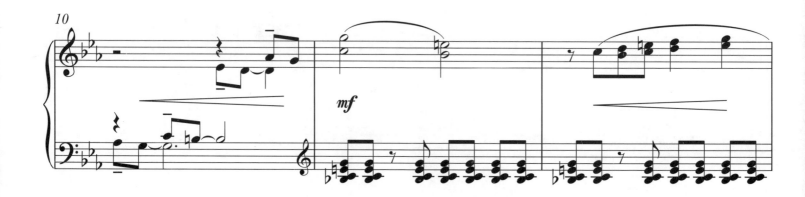

The Party On The Wisla from 'Trois Couleurs Blanc'

Composed by Zbigniew Preisner
Arranged by Jack Long

© Copyright 1993 by MK2 - 55, rue Traversière - 75012 Paris - France.
This arrangement © Copyright 2004 by MK2.
All Rights Reserved. International Copyright Secured.

Fashion Show I from 'Trois Couleurs Rouge'

Composed by Zbigniew Preisner
Arranged by Jack Long

© Copyright 1994 by MK2 - 55, rue Traversière - 75012 Paris - France.
This arrangement © Copyright 2004 by MK2.
All Rights Reserved. International Copyright Secured.

Do Not Take Another Man's Wife I from 'Trois Couleurs Rouge'

Composed by Zbigniew Preisner
Arranged by Jack Long

© Copyright 1989 Amplitude Editions Musicales SARL.
This arrangement © Copyright 2004 by Amplitude Editions Musicales SARL.
All Rights Reserved. International Copyright Secured.

Fashion Show II from 'Trois Couleurs Rouge'

Composed by Zbigniew Preisner
Arranged by Jack Long

© Copyright 1994 by MK2 - 55, rue Traversière - 75012 Paris - France.
This arrangement © Copyright 2004 by MK2.
All Rights Reserved. International Copyright Secured.

Finale from 'Trois Couleurs Rouge'

Composed by Zbigniew Preisner
Arranged by Jack Long

© Copyright 1994 by MK2 - 55, rue Traversière - 75012 Paris - France.
This arrangement © Copyright 2004 by MK2.
All Rights Reserved. International Copyright Secured.

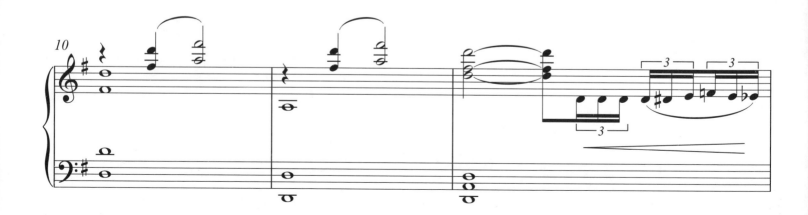

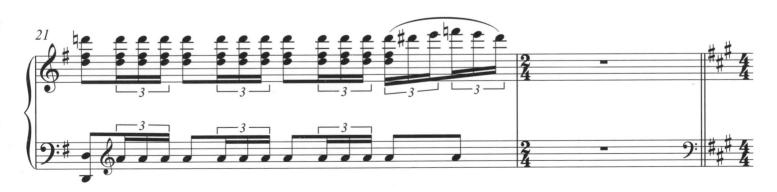

Published by
Chester Music
8/9 Frith Street, London W1D 3JB, England.

Exclusive distributors:
Music Sales Limited
Distribution Centre, Newmarket Road, Bury St. Edmunds,
Suffolk IP33 3YB, England.

Music Sales Corporation
257 Park Avenue South, New York, NY10010,
United States of America.

Music Sales Pty Limited
120 Rothschild Avenue, Rosebery,
NSW 2018, Australia.

Order No. CH68200
ISBN 1-84449-548-5
This book © Copyright 2004 by Chester Music.

Unauthorised reproduction of any part of this
publication by any means including photocopying is
an infringement of copyright.

Music arrangements by Jack Long
(except 'Home At Last' and 'Morning At The Hotel'
by Quentin Thomas).
Music processed by Camden Music.
Compiled by Laurence Aston.
Edited by Christopher Hussey.

Printed in the United Kingdom.

www.musicsales.com

The soundtrack for this film trilogy is available for sale.
Please visit the website www.mk2.com

Your Guarantee of Quality:
As publishers, we strive to produce every book to
the highest commercial standards.
Whilst endeavouring to retain the original running
order of the recorded albums, the book has been carefully
designed to minimise awkward page turns and to
make playing from it a real pleasure.
Particular care has been given to specifying acid-free,
neutral-sized paper made from pulps which have not
been elemental chlorine bleached.
This pulp is from farmed sustainable forests and was
produced with special regard for the environment.
Throughout, the printing and binding have been
planned to ensure a sturdy, attractive publication which
should give years of enjoyment.
If your copy fails to meet our high standards, please
inform us and we will gladly replace it.